50 Classical Guitar Pieces

In Tablature
and Standard Notation

Arranged, Edited and Fingered by Joseph Harris

Catalog #07-4052

ISBN 978-1-56922-080-1

Printed in Canada

Cover Photo by James Bean, Ojai, California
Classical Guitar by Robert Ruck
Courtesy of Classic Guitars International
Sherman Oaks, California
Guitar Book Produced by John L. Haag

Exclusive Distributor for the Entire World:
CREATIVE CONCEPTS PUBLISHING CORPORATION
6020-B Nicolle Street, Ventura, California 93003
Check out our Web site at *http://www.creativeconcepts.com* or you can Email us at *mail@creativeconcepts.com*

50 Classical Guitar Pieces

◆◆ ◆◆ ◆◆ ◆◆ ◆◆ ◆◆ ◆◆ ◆◆ ◆◆ CONTENTS ◆◆ ◆◆ ◆◆ ◆◆ ◆◆ ◆◆ ◆◆ ◆◆ ◆◆

50 Classical Guitar Pieces

◆◆ ◆◆ ◆◆ ◆◆ ◆◆ ◆◆ ◆◆ ◆◆ ◆◆ **CONTENTS** ◆◆ ◆◆ ◆◆ ◆◆ ◆◆ ◆◆ ◆◆ ◆◆ ◆◆

◆◆ THE CLASSICAL ERA ◆◆ ◆◆ ◆◆ ◆◆ ◆◆ ◆◆ ◆◆ ◆◆ ◆◆ ◆◆ ◆◆ ◆◆ ◆◆

◆◆ THE ROMANTIC ERA ◆◆ ◆◆ ◆◆ ◆◆ ◆◆ ◆◆ ◆◆ ◆◆ ◆◆ ◆◆ ◆◆ ◆◆ ◆◆

Historical Notes/Performance Suggestions

The Renaissance Era

Vincenzo Galilei (c.1520-1591)
Saltarello

Although today we more easily remember the accomplishments of his father, the great astronomer and physicist Galileo Galilei, Italian musician and scholar Vincenzo Galilei held a significant role in the evolution of music, one that would dramatically alter the course of Western music forever. Galilei was a key member of a small group of musicians called the Florentine Camerata, historically informed scholars who wished to inject the music of their time with the simplicity of ancient Greek music. The publication which most clearly describes Galilei's musical views is his *Discorso sopra la musica antica et moderna* (1581). Galilei's own compositions for solo voice and lute, with clear textures consisting of a naturally declamated vocal line and an unobtrusive chordal accompaniment, helped form the musical blueprint for what would later be called the monodic style and eventually lead to the birth of opera.

Galilei's demand for musical clarity extended to solo performance on the lute, an instrument he was quite proficient on and for which he composed many works. Galilei was opposed to the then-common practice of enlarging the range of stringed instruments through the addition of extra strings, which sometimes resulted in an instrument with as many as sixteen strings!

The Saltarello in D Major (found on page 13) enjoyed a rebirth in the twentieth century after being lost for three hundred years. It was discovered and transcribed from a sixteenth-century codex of anonymous works by Italian musicologist Oscar Chilesotti (1848-1916), who was quick to attribute the piece to Galilei, most likely due to an already large number of pieces by Galilei with that title. When playing the Saltarello on the modern guitar, a particular aim will be to keep the melody clear and singing. Also, be careful that the drone of the bass strings does not overpower the melody.

Pierre Attaingnant (c.1494-1552)
Pavane; Gaillarde; La Brosse

Pierre Attaingnant was an innovator in the field of music publishing. In 1529 he created the earliest known documents of French lute tablature. He was also the first music publisher in France to employ movable type. Attaingnant's method of simultaneously printing staff segments and notes proved to be a vast improvement over the older method of printing staff lines and note heads in separate passes. This new method virtually cut printing time (and costs) in half. Attaingnant's publications include seven books of masses, thirteen books of motets, and 35 books of chansons.

Although published under his name, it is uncertain whether the individual pieces in Attaingnant's *18 Basses Danses* (1529) were actually composed by him. Next to the titles of some of the pieces is the inscription "P.B.," which may intend authorship by lutenist Pierre Blondeau, who was in the employ of Attaingnant as an editor. During the Renaissance, it was common in performance to pair a pavane with a galliarde. The Pavane and Gaillarde included in this book (see pages 14 and 15, respectively) contain striking thematic similarities and most certainly must have been intended to have been performed together. The Pavane should be played in a slow, stately manner, while the Gaillarde should be lively and sprightly. The title of La Brosse (found on page 16) is most likely a reference to a particular individual whose identity unfortunately remains unknown to us today. Keep the piece in a moderately quick tempo and play with a strong tone.

Adrian Le Roy (c.1520-1598)
Passemeze

With his partner Robert Ballard, Adrian Le Roy succeeded Pierre Attaingnant as the most important and powerful French publisher and one of the most important music publishers in history. Through his role as artistic leader of the Parisian publishing houses, Le Roy held a firm grip in the shaping of French musical tastes. He was friends with many of the most distinguished composers of the day, including Claude Le Jeune, Jacob Aracadelt, Pierre Certon, and most significantly the Italian composer Orlando di Lasso. Le Roy was pen-pal to Lasso for many years and tried in vain to gain a musical post for his friend in France. In addition to being a publisher, Le Roy was also a composer, pedagogue, theorist and performer on stringed instruments such as the lute and the cittern.

The Passemeze (found on page 17) is a dance piece and should played be in a quick and lively tempo. Since the modern guitar is a much more resonant instrument than the sixteenth-century lute, you may have to take special care that certain notes, especially those on open strings, do not sustain for too long into the next chord.

Anonymous
Greensleeves; Kemp's Jig; Watkin's Ale; Wilson's Wilde; Danza

During the Renaissance, many English folk tunes enjoyed arrangements for solo lute. Perhaps the most famous English folk tune of the time is Greensleeves (found on page 18). One popular arrangement was in *William Ballet's Lute Book* (1580), a compilation of Elizabethan lute music done by various persons at different times. Kemp's Jig (found on page 19), Watkin's Ale (found on page 20) and Wilson's Wilde (found on page 22) are other popular lute arrangements. The pieces should all sound energetic and dance-like in performance.

The Danza in E Minor (found on page 23) is from an anonymous Italian source. When performing the Danza, keep the tempo at a moderately fast pace, without letting the chordal passages sound too choppy.

The Baroque Era

Gaspar Sanz (1640-1710)
Rujero; Canarios; Españoleta

Gaspar Sanz was a musician and a scholar whose works inspired the people in his native Spain for many years. Sanz held degrees in theology and philosophy from the University at Salamanca, Spain. He traveled to Italy, where he met and studied with many musicians including guitarist Francesco Corbetta. Sanz's *Instrucción de Música sobre la Guitarra Española* (1674) is a veritable cornucopia of examples of contemporary Spanish dances and folk songs. The book also explains practical issues such as *rasgueado* (strumming), *punteado* (plucking) and *alfabeto* (a shorthand method for the notation of chords). Sanz's treatise was the most comprehensive work of its kind at the time and became very popular in Spain. The great twentieth-century Spanish composer Joaquín Rodrigo's *Fantasia para un Gentilhombre* (1954) for guitar and orchestra is a pastiche of Sanz's melodies.

Three of Sanz's examples of contemporary Spanish dances are contained in this book. Since they are dances, they should all exhibit a lively character and maintain an even tempo.

Robert de Visée (c.1650-c.1725)
Menuet; Menuet; Menuet; Gavotte; Sarabande; Bourrée

Louis XIV's court at Versailles was a model of elegance. Louis was an avid patron of the arts; his court held constant celebrations of theater, dance (Louis himself was a fine dancer, dancing in some of the ballet productions at the court) and especially music. Robert de Visée was one of many musicians at the employ of the court and was involved in many aspects of courtly music making. As well as providing daily guitar instruction to Louis, Visée entertained the court upon the guitar, lute, theorbo and viol in both chamber groups and solo performances. In the evenings, Visée and his guitar were often called upon to provide a soothing soporific for the King while he lay in bed.

Visée published at least three books of guitar music: *Livre de guitarre dédie au roy* (1682), *Livre de pièces pour la guitarre* (1686) and *Troisième livre de pièces pour la guitarre* (1689). Most of Visée's pieces for the guitar are to be found in the form of suites, which are collections of various dances. The dance pieces of Visée found in this book should sound very graceful and elegant. Perform the ornaments light and quick, and make sure that the contrapuntal interplay between the voices remains clear.

Bernardo Pasquini (1637-1710)
Aria

Bernardo Pasquini was the most important Italian composer of keyboard music during the latter half of the seventeenth century. Pasquini was highly esteemed by his contemporaries and during his lifetime was believed to be the greatest performer in Italy.

The Aria (found on page 37) is today most well-known through its arrangement by Ottorino Respighi in his orchestral suite *The Birds* (1927). When performing the Aria on guitar, keep the tempo even and stately, and play with a strong attack and a full tone.

Elisabeth-Claude Jacquet de la Guerre (c.1664-1729)
Menuet

Elisabeth-Claude Jacquet de la Guerre was a French harpsichordist, organist, and composer. She was a precociously gifted child, exhibiting talents as an excellent sight-reader, improviser and performer. Jacquet's skills were recognized and encouraged by Louis XIV. Her published works include the five-act opera *Cephale et Procris* (1694), two books of cantatas and various chamber works.

The Menuet (found on page 38) is from Jacquet's *Pièces de claveçin* (1687) and like most French Baroque keyboard music is heavily loaded with ornamentation. To prevent the meter from becoming too obscured, be sure to begin each ornament directly on the downbeat.

Jean-François Dandrieu (c.1682-1738)
Gavotte en rondeau

Jean-François Dandrieu was an organist, composer and one of the most celebrated harpsichordists of the eighteenth century. From 1733 until his death he was employed as organist at Saint-Barthélemy in Paris. Among his works are *Principes de l'accompagnement du clavecin* (c.1719), three books of clavecin pieces and many nöels (Christmas songs or carols) for organ.

Dandrieu's keyboard compositions show a predilection for rondeau form. The form of the rondeau is simple. The piece begins with a statement of the rondeau theme, usually repeated in performance. This is immediately followed by the first couplet, then a restatement of the rondeau theme. Next comes the second couplet, and so on, concluding with a final statement of the rondeau theme. The Gavotte en rondeau (found on page 40) exhibits a regular static bass and a lively melody, characteristics of another French dance, the tambourin. Special care must be taken in the Gavotte en rondeau that the open bass strings in the accompaniment do not drown out the melody.

Antonio Vivaldi (1675-1741)
Allegro non molto; Sarabanda

For many years remembered only for his numerous violin concertos, Antonio Vivaldi is recognized today as a key musical figure of the Italian Baroque. Although his most visible and enduring influence was indeed in the development of the solo concerto, Vivaldi was admired in his day as an excellent composer of chamber music, a stunning violinist and a popular composer of Italian opera. Exhibiting an apparent ease of composition (he once boasted he could compose a piece faster than it could be copied), Vivaldi proved to be extremely prolific, composing over 50 operas, 90 sonatas and 450 concertos. This composer of "The Four Seasons" was a bold and impetuous individual who managed to focus his musical impulses in a unique voice that was consistent yet always expressive.

Vivaldi's Concertos for Violin, Op. 8 were first published in 1725 and dedicated to the Bohemian Count Wenzeslaus von Morzin. The first four concertos, collectively known as "The Four Seasons," are programmatic. The score for each concerto includes an explanatory sonnet, perhaps written by Vivaldi himself. Specific lines of poetry correspond to particular passages in the music. In the *Allegro non molto* from Concerto No. 2 (found on page 42), sustain the chords for as long as possible, releasing with the left hand at the last possible moment. Keep the tempo even without letting it drag. Apply liberal amounts of vibrato and roll chords with the right hand as little as possible. When performing this short movement, be thinking about the lines from the sonnet Vivaldi inserted into the score: "In this season of the blazing sun, man and flock swelter while the pines are seared."

The *Sarabanda* (found on page 44) contains a *petite reprise,* a formal device borrowed from the French in which a short phrase is repeated. This short passage is heard three times in performance, so be sure to perform it differently each time. To give this Italian sarabanda the proper lilt, accent the second beat of each measure, as you would with a French sarabande.

Giovanni Zamboni (late 1600s-early 1700s)
Preludio

Giovanni Zamboni, a native of Rome, was a virtuoso on several instruments including the lute, theorbo, harpsichord, chitarra sminuita (a small version of the modern guitar), mandore and mandolin. In regards to his compositional skills, he was praised by one of his contemporaries as being an "excellent contrapuntist." In addition to compositions for the lute, Zamboni's known publications include two books of madrigals for four voices and basso continuo. Zamboni earned a living working as a jeweler and as a musician at the Pisa Cathedral.

One of the scant surviving documents concerning Zamboni's life describes a brawl during Mass with Giovanni Gelli, a Florentine musician also working at the Pisa Cathedral. Immediately after communion, the two musicians became engaged in a heated argument which led to the challenge of a duel with swords. While still inside the Cathedral, the two came to blows, but fortunately someone intervened and stopped the fight before the two could hurt each other. Peace was made and the two became friends as before.

Zamboni's *Sonate d'intavolatura di leuto* was published in Lucca, Italy in 1718. The Preludio (found on page 46) is written in an improvisatory style and features a variety of textures, motives and phrase lengths.

J.S. Bach (1685-1750)
Prelude; Bourrée, Chorale, Sarabande; Sarabande; Musette

Johann Sebastian Bach represents the musical culmination of the Baroque style. As a composer, Bach was a master of nearly every Baroque genre (the only major exception being opera). Bach was a musical sponge; he absorbed ideas from all the music he heard, regardless of nationality or style, and redirected these ideas outwards in his own music. It is ironic that although Bach is cherished today as one of the most magnificent composers of all time, he did not enjoy widespread fame during his lifetime; his contemporaries generally recognized him only as a fine organist and a crafty contrapuntist.

Bach composed at least seven works for the lute, including four complete dance suites. The Prelude for Lute (found on page 50) is a stand-alone piece, and is not associated with any other works. The Bourrée (found on page 54) is a favorite among beginning guitarists. The piece actually contains many deceptively difficult passages (most notably mm. 22-25), so be sure to choose a starting tempo that is not too fast for the rest of the piece.

The sarabande is a Baroque dance characterized by a slow tempo and an accent on the second beat. Both of the Bach sarabandes included in this book (found on pages 56 and 58) should be kept slow and stately.

The Musette in D Major (found on page 62) should sound simple and rustic in character. The open bass notes give the piece its special character, and recall the musette, a small French bagpipe.

Play the Chorale from Cantata No. 67 (found on page 49) in a slow, relaxed manner. Use as much flesh of the fingertip as possible with an aim to keep all notes of each chord at an equal dynamic level.

George Frideric Handel (1685-1759)
Sarabande

George Frideric Handel is considered a "cosmopolitan" composer. He was born in Halle, Germany and spent a great part of his formative years traveling throughout Europe (with significant stops in Naples, Rome, Venice, Paris and London). As a consequence, Handel's style is an amalgam of German, Italian, French and English influences. Since all of Handel's mature life was spent in London and all the works for which he is chiefly remembered were written for English audiences, he is regarded by some as being stylistically an English composer. Unlike his close contemporary J.S. Bach, Handel was internationally renowned in his lifetime. Handel's first opera *Almira*, produced in Hamburg in 1705, brought him immediate fame.

Handel's keyboard compositions are undeservedly overshadowed by the enduring popularity of his vocal works. The Sarabande (found on page 64) comes from a Partita for solo keyboard written early in Handel's career, some time before 1705. Handel's keyboard works are marked by symmetrical formal outlines and Italianate influences. Ornamentation, a hallmark of the French style, is kept to a minimum.

The Classical Era

Matteo Carcassi (1792-1853)
Prelude; Andantino; Study

The Italian guitarist Matteo Carcassi was born in Florence, but lived most of his mature musical life in Paris, making occasional side trips to England and Germany. Carcassi was fortunate that he happened upon the French guitar scene at the right time. The aging Italian guitar virtuoso Ferdinando Carulli had fallen out of favor with French audiences, who found in the young Carcassi a fresh, energetic approach to the instrument. As can be evinced from his *Méthode complète pour la guitarre* (1840), Carcassi was a master of the technical capabilities of the guitar. In the book, Carcassi explains the rudiments of guitar technique (chords, scales, arpeggios, etc.), more advanced techniques of musical expression (slurs, tremolo and vibrato) and newly-discovered special effects *(sons etouffés)*. Carcassi's *Méthode* was quite comprehensive in scope. In addition to guitar-specific information, the book includes discussions on music theory, musical terms and even guitar construction. The *Méthode* proved to be one of the most popular guitar method books for many decades, all the way into the late twentieth century.

In addition to his studies, for which he is primarily known today, Carcassi composed many fantasias and variations, as well as dozens of shorter works such as rondos and waltzes. The Prelude in C Major (found on page 69) is a very short arpeggio study. Shorter pieces like this and the Andantino in C Major (found on page 66) make good exercises in tone production. Once the notes are mastered, work on making each individual note sound as rich and full as possible. The Study in A Minor (found on page 67) exercises two major technical issues: tremolo (as seen in the opening measure) and arpeggios (as seen in mm. 2-4). Strive to maintain a dynamic and metrical equality between these two musical ideas, so that each flows seamlessly into the other.

Dionisio Aguado (1784-1849)
Study

The Spaniard Dionisio Aguado was a good friend and musical companion to his fellow countryman and guitarist Fernando Sor. Aguado and Sor were roommates in Paris for many years and sometimes performed in concert together. Their friendship must have been a strong bond indeed, for they remained friends and musical partners even though each possessed a distinctly different approach to guitar technique. While Aguado preferred the use of his fingernails when plucking the strings of the guitar, Sor held to a practice more common at the time, that of keeping one's fingernails very short so that only the flesh of the right hand touched the strings. The difference in sound between the two players was great. Aguado's tone was very crisp and penetrating; however, Sor's tone was mellow yet still powerful. Aguado would ultimately confess late in life that he regretted his choice to use his fingernails. Unfortunately, by that time it was too late for him to change his technique.

Aguado's works for the guitar comprise a vast number of charming miniatures: 45 waltzes, six minuets and numerous rondos, dances and fantasias. His didactic interests are obvious from his

Colección de Estudios para Guitarra (1820) and *Nuevo Método para Guitarra* (1843). The Study in A Minor (found on page 70) is a charming and simple study in arpeggio playing. Since the piece is technically undemanding, possibilities for expressive interpretation are limitless. The real trick of the Study is to create a unique musical atmosphere while focusing on a perfect technique and steady meter.

Fernando Sor (1778-1839)
Minuet; Leçon; Leçon; Petite Pièce; Petite Pièce ; Study

Fernando Sor is an outstanding figurehead in the history of the guitar in Spain. Sor composed music for a variety of media, but is chiefly remembered today for his contributions to guitar repertoire, which include sonatas, variations, divertimenti, minuets, studies, and even a treatise on guitar playing. What sets apart Sor's treatise from the dozens of others written around the same time is his rational approach to musical matters. Sor emphasized in his treatise that all compositional and technical concerns should serve a fundamental musical purpose. The guitar works of Sor are noteworthy for their varieties of textures, impeccable voice-leading and an attention to cantabile style melodic writing.

Although Sor has been referred to as "the Beethoven of the guitar," his music is very classical in character; instead of a heightened sense of musical drama, his music exhibits elegance and harmonic and formal clarity, hallmarks of the classical style. The pieces by Sor contained in this book should be performed with these goals in mind. Above all, at all times, make sure that the melody is clear, distinct, and sings.

The Romantic Era

Francisco Tárrega (1852-1909)
Study; Lágrima (Preludio) ; Adelita (Mazurca); María (Gavota)

Through his achievements in guitar technique, transcription and composition, Francisco Tárrega ushered the guitar into the twentieth century, paving the way for future masters of the instrument like Andrés Segovia to elevate the status of the guitar to that of a noble concert instrument.

Three of the selections of Tárrega included in this volume are short character pieces, quite typical of Tárrega's output. Each exhibits a unique, individual musical character in a very short span of time. In Làgrima (found on page 84), perform the melody as singing as possible. Be careful that every note is held for its full duration, especially in chordal passages (such as m.10).

In Adelita (found on page 85), make sure that the accompaniment never overpowers the melody. For example, in the first measure make sure that the chord on beat three is quieter than the half note B in the melody. In mm. 13-14, the melody travels to the bass voice. Here, perform all the notes in the low register with the thumb, but roll the notes slightly and accent the melody notes with thumb rest strokes.

María (found on page 86) is a character piece written in the form of a stylized dance, an eighteenth-century gavotte. The gavotte is characterized by its two upbeats (here represented by two eighth notes) and strong downbeat at the beginning of the measure. In order to retain a dance-like character, the meter must remain even throughout; however, an occasional application of rubato for expressive purposes would not be out of line. The grace notes should be performed very light and quick. Strike the grace note with a little extra force, but ease up left hand pressure during the slide so that the goal note sounds very elegant and unostentatious. Play the pizzicato passage at the end entirely with the thumb of the right hand. To produce the muffled sound of the pizzicato, rest the heel of the hand very close to the bridge. Shift the placement of the right hand during the passage to ensure that all the notes receive an equal amount of pizzicato.

The Study in C Major (found on page 83) is a simple study in arpeggio playing. Hang on to the notes of each chord for as long as possible, letting go of them only at the barline.

P. José Antonio de Donostía (1886-1957)
Canción Triste

Padre José Antonio de Donostía (1886-1957) was a Franciscan monk at San Sebastián, a city in the Basque region of northern Spain. Donostía is recognized as one of the foremost authorities on Basque folk music and has published several important books on the subject. The *Preludios Vascos* ("Basque Preludes") are a set of short pieces for the piano that express the character of the Basque region through musical suggestion, rather than by utilizing actual Basque melodies.

The *Preludios* are character pieces in the truest sense of the term. They are short, in simple structures and each evocative of a single unique mood. Regarding the *Preludios,* Donostía himself acknowledged an indebtedness to Robert Schumann, the quintessential composer of the Romantic character piece. When playing these pieces, try to be aware of the atmosphere you are evoking. The colorful, impressionistic harmonies in Canción Triste ("Song of Sadness;" found on page 89) lie so well on the guitar that it may seem surprising this piece was originally intended for piano. In order to emulate the resonance of the piano, hold on to the chords for as long as possible. A good trick is to give each chord a quick squeeze with the left hand immediately before release. Moving inner voices in the musical texture should be clear without overpowering the main melody in the upper voice. Special care should be taken in the *tranquilo* section (mm. 45-52) that each voice remain rhythmically and melodically distinct. This passage should also be played with a contrasting tone color. Using as much flesh of the fingertip as possible will produce a rich, dark Brahmsian tone.

Anonymous
Romanza; El Noi de la Mare; El Mestre

The folk music of Spain has been a source of inspiration to composers and performers for centuries. Romanza (found on page 94) is a popular piece that has enjoyed immense popularity as an arpeggio study. For this piece, accent the melody notes and apply vibrato liberally. "El Noi de la Mare" ("The Mother's Infant Child;" found on page 96) should sound like a lullaby. Keep the meter gently rocking, and imagine the melody in very long, fluid phrases. "El Mestre" ("The Master;" found on page 98) is a folk tune from the Catalan region in northern Spain. When the melody is in the low register (as in mm. 19-20), use thumb rest strokes to help to bring out the melody. When the thumb strikes more than one note at a time (as in m. 20), "roll" the chord slightly and give the melody note a bit more stress. In passages with artificial harmonics (as in mm. 23-28), play the harmonics with as much force as possible, while being careful to play the accompanying notes at an equal volume.

About the Arranger

Joseph Harris received his bachelor's and master's degrees in guitar performance at Northern Arizona University as a student of Tom Sheeley. Joseph has done further graduate study in music theory at the University of Iowa. In addition to his work with the classical guitar, his musical pursuits include jazz guitar, music aesthetics and the music of French composer Olivier Messiaen (1908-1992). In his spare time Joseph enjoys camping, canoeing, spelunking and rock climbing.

Saltarello in D Major

Arranged for guitar by
Joseph Harris

Vincenzo Galilei
(1520–1591)

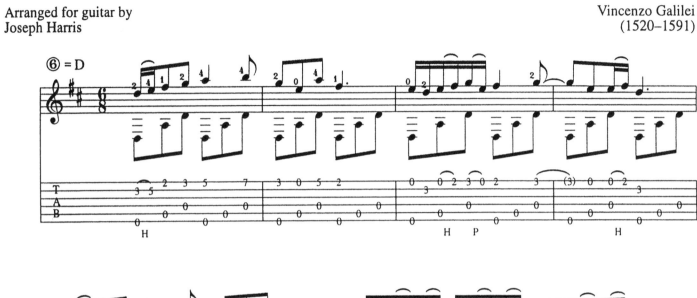

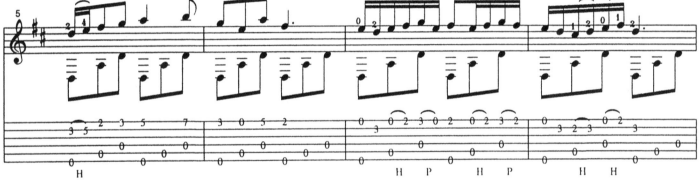

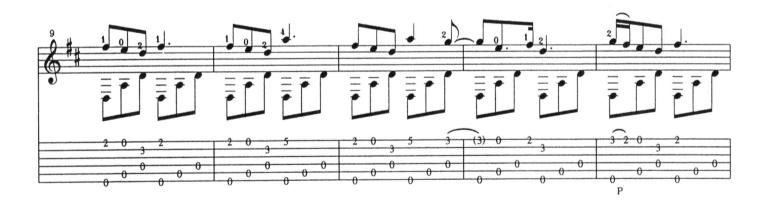

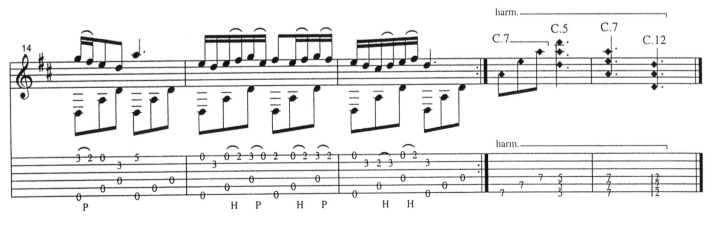

Pavane
from *18 Basses Danses* (1529)

Arranged for guitar by
Joseph Harris

Pierre Attaingnant
(c.1480–1552)

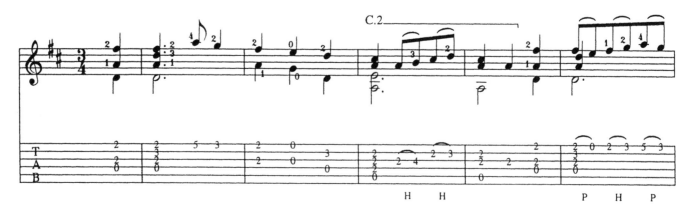

Gaillarde
from *18 Basses Danses* (1529)

Arranged for guitar by
Joseph Harris

Pierre Attaingnant
(c.1480–1552)

La Brosse

from *18 Basses Danses* (1529)

Arranged for guitar by
Joseph Harris

Pierre Attaingnant
(c.1480–1552)

Passemeze
from *A Briefe and Easye Instruction* (1568)

Arranged for guitar by
Joseph Harris

Adrian Le Roy
(1520–1598)

Greensleeves

Arranged for guitar by
Joseph Harris

Anonymous

Kemp's Jig

Arranged for guitar by
Joseph Harris

Anonymous

Watkin's Ale

Arranged for guitar by
Joseph Harris

Anonymous

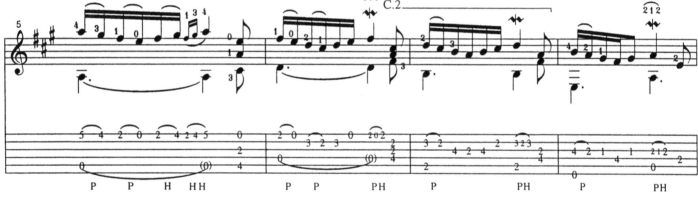

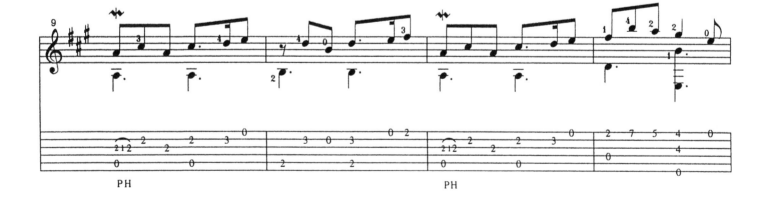

Wilson's Wilde

Arranged for guitar by
Joseph Harris

Anonymous

Danza in E Minor

Arranged for guitar by
Joseph Harris

Anonymous

Rujero
from *Instrucción de Música sobre la Guitarra Española* (1674)

Edited and fingered by
Joseph Harris

Gaspar Sanz
(1640–1710)

Canarios
from *Instrucción de Música sobre la Guitarra Española* (1674)

Edited and fingered by
Joseph Harris

Gaspar Sanz
(1640–1710)

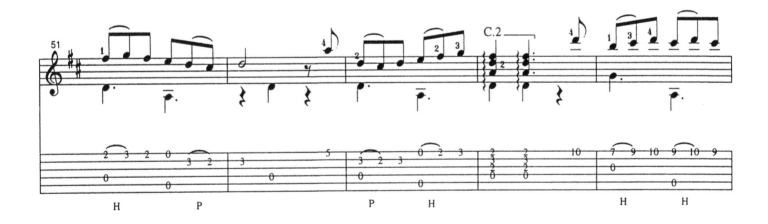

Españoletas
from *Instrucción de Música sobre la Guitarra Española* (1674)

Edited and fingered by
Joseph Harris

Gaspar Sanz
(1640–1710)

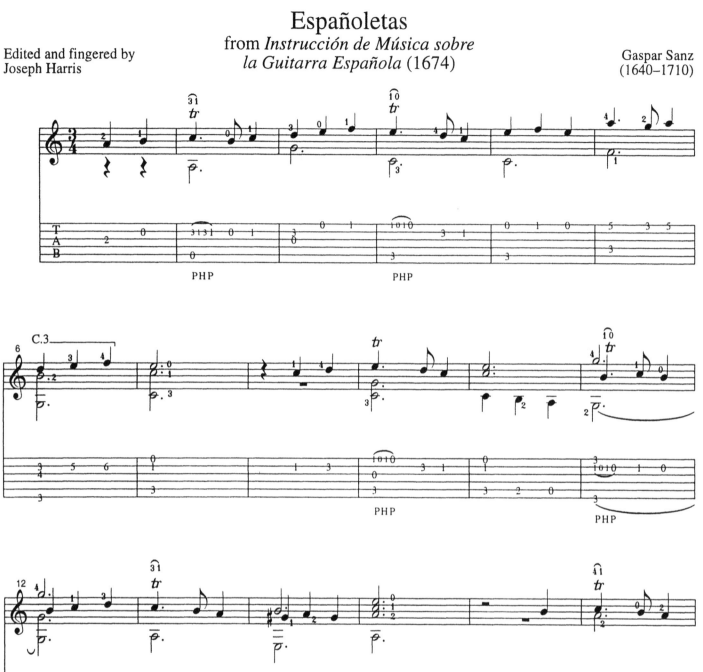

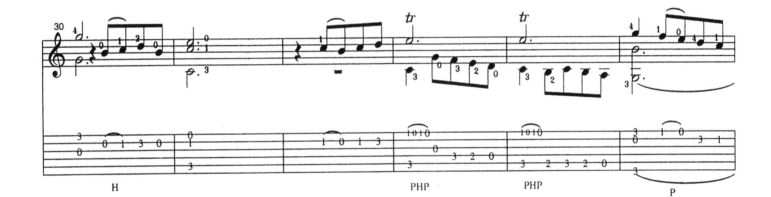

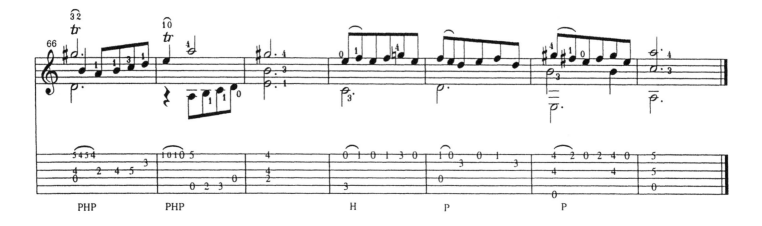

Menuet in E Minor

Edited and fingered by
Joseph Harris

Robert de Visée
(c.1650–c.1725)

Menuet in D Major

Arranged for guitar by
Joseph Harris

Robert de Visée
(c.1650–c.1725)

Menuet in D Minor

Arranged for guitar by
Joseph Harris

Robert de Visée
(c.1650–c.1725)

Gavotte

Edited and fingered by
Joseph Harris

Robert de Visée
(c.1650–c.1725)

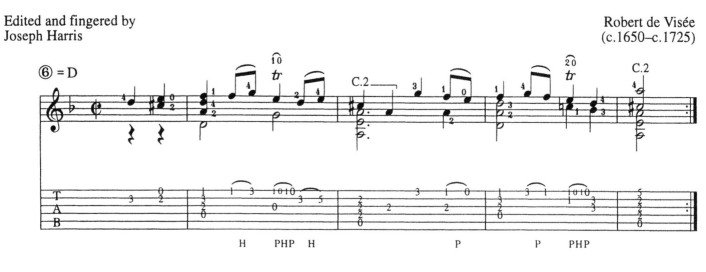

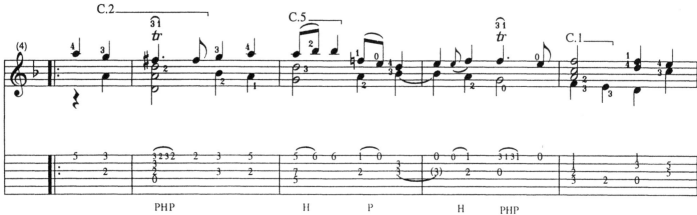

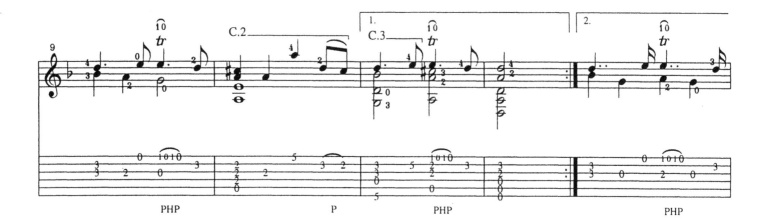

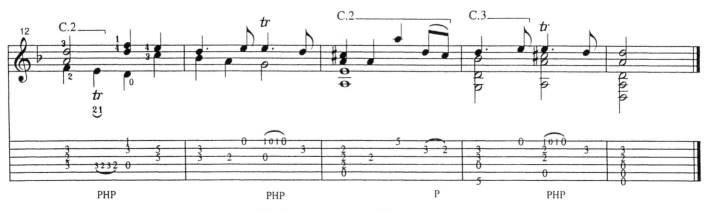

Sarabande in D Minor

Edited and fingered by
Joseph Harris

Robert de Visée
(c.1650–c.1725)

Bourrée in D Minor

Arranged for guitar by
Joseph Harris

Robert de Visée
(c.1650–c.1710)

Aria

Arranged for guitar
by Joseph Harris

Bernardo Pasquini
(1637-1710)

Menuet
from *Pièces de clavecin* (1687)

Arranged for guitar
by Joseph Harris

Elisabeth-Claude Jacquet de la Guerre
(c.1664-1729)

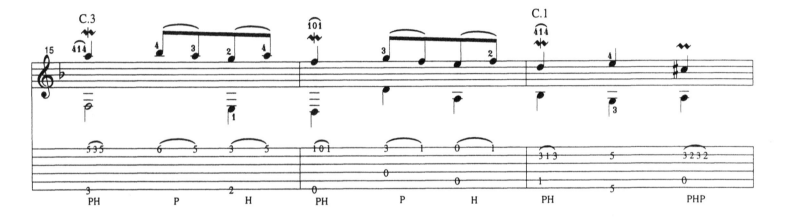

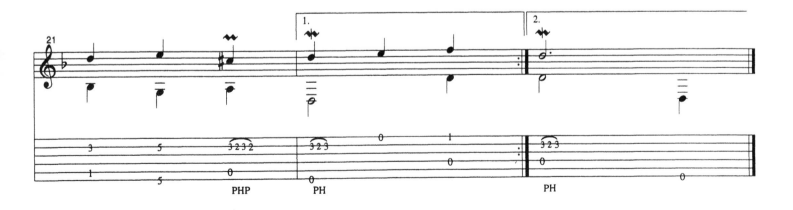

Gavotte en rondeau

Arranged for guitar
by Joseph Harris

Jean François Dandrieu
(1682-1738)

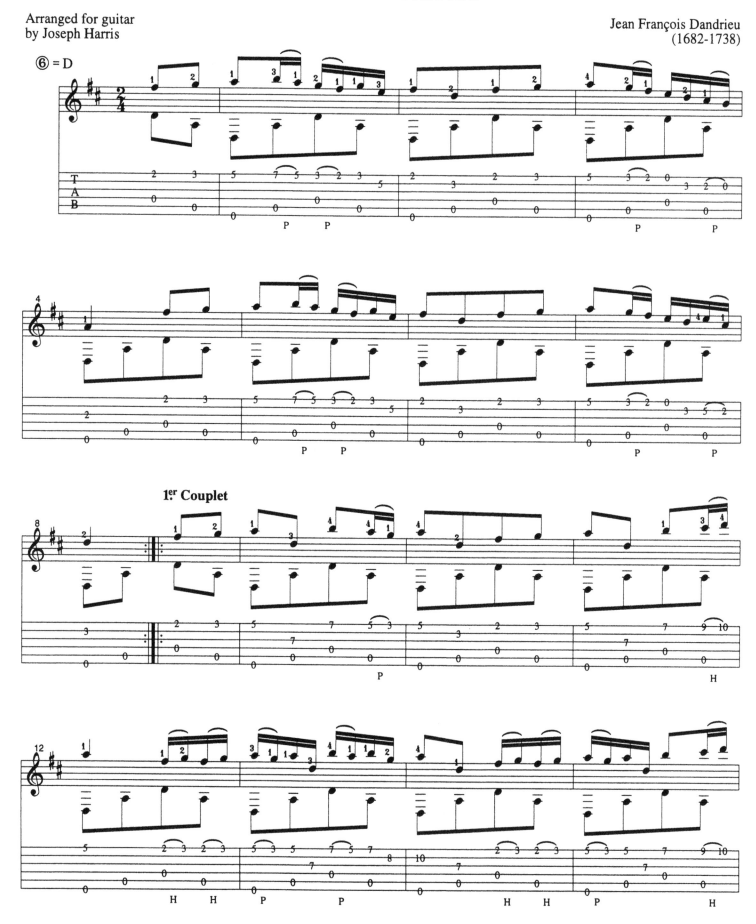

41

2.ᵉ Couplet

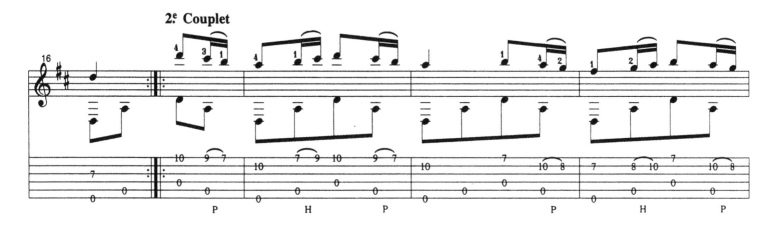

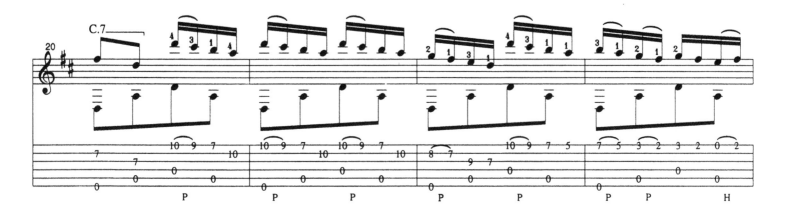

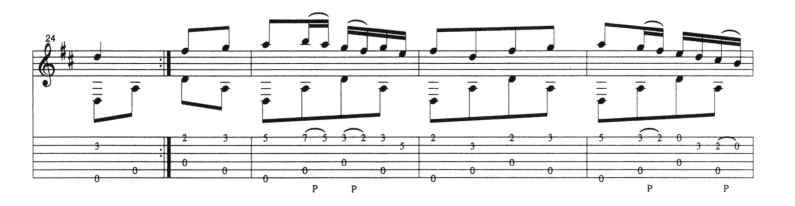

Allegro non molto
from *The Four Seasons,* Op. 8, No. 2 ("Summer")

Arranged for guitar by
Joseph Harris

Antonio Vivaldi
(1678-1741)

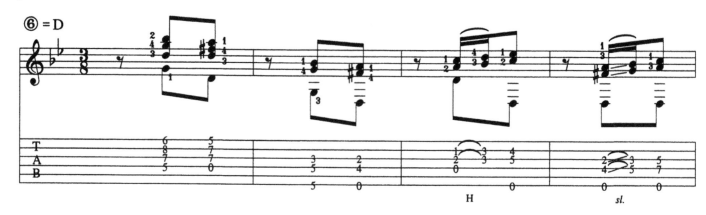

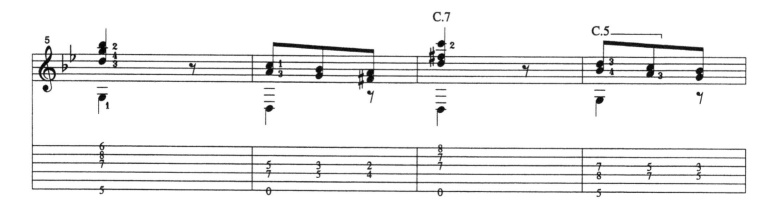

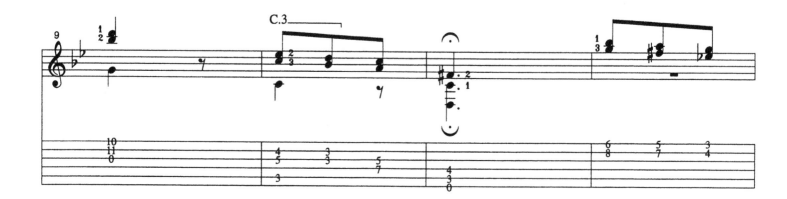

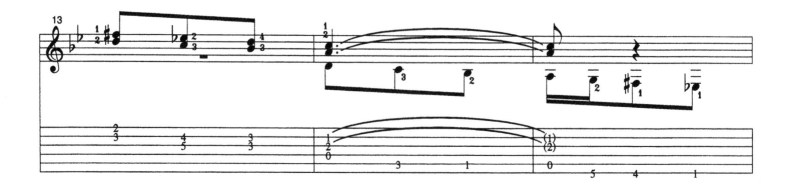

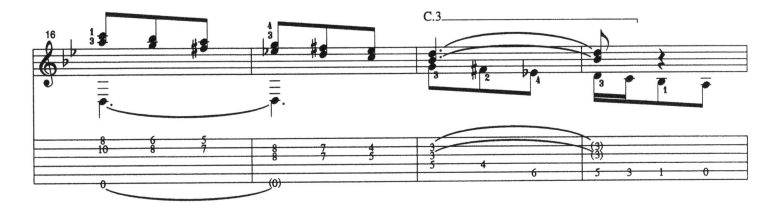

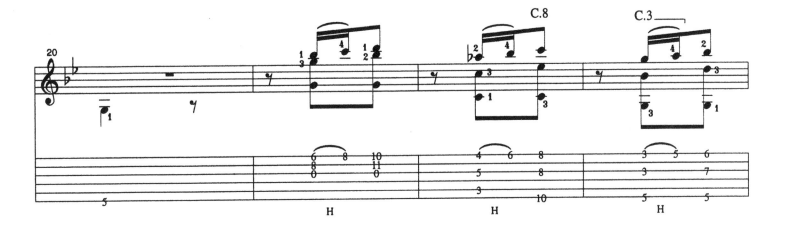

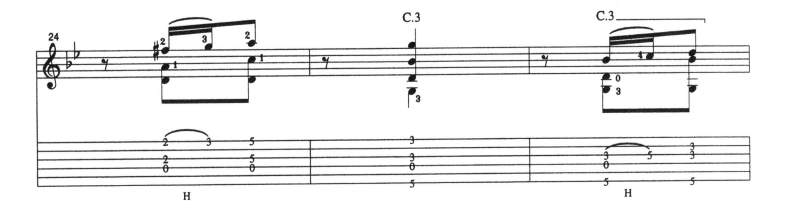

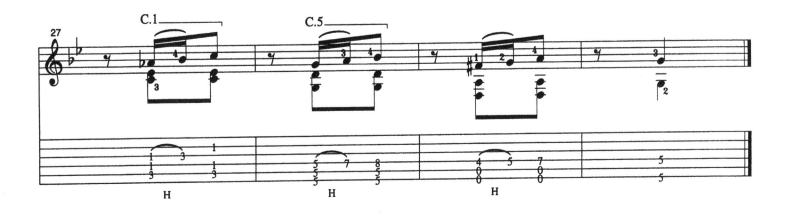

Sarabanda
from Sonata for Flute, RV 49

Arranged for guitar by
Joseph Harris

Antonio Vivaldi
(1678-1741)

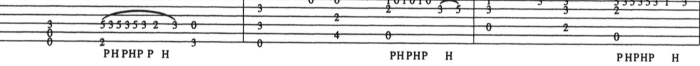

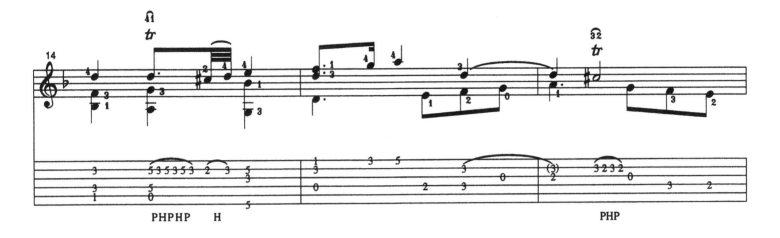

Preludio
from *Sonate d'intavolatura de leuto,* Opus 1

Arranged for guitar
by Joseph Harris

Giovanni Zamboni
(late 1600s-early 1700s)

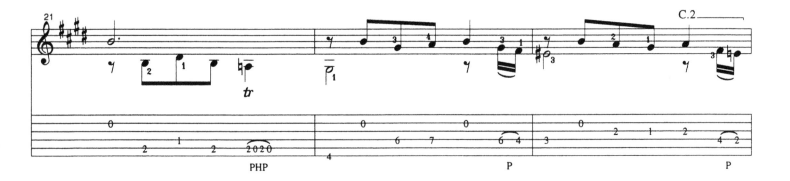

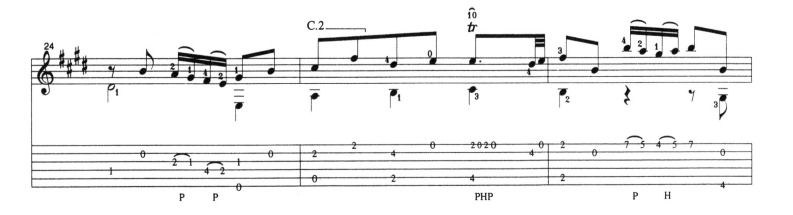

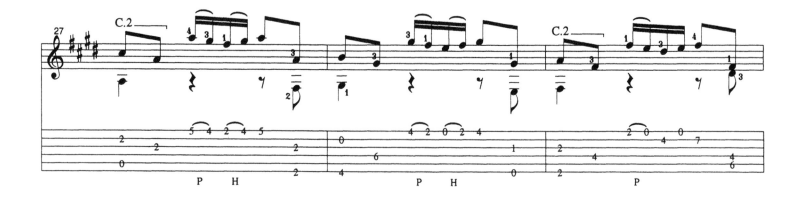

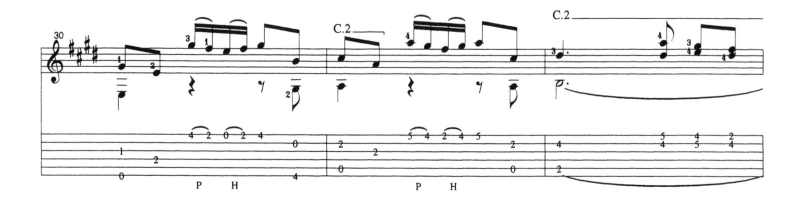

Chorale
from Cantata No. 67, *"Du Friedenfürst, Herr Jesu Christ"*

Arranged for guitar by
Joseph Harris

J.S. Bach
(1685-1750)

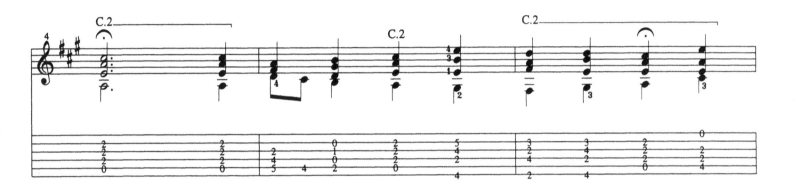

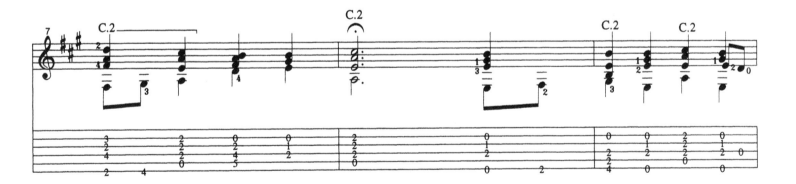

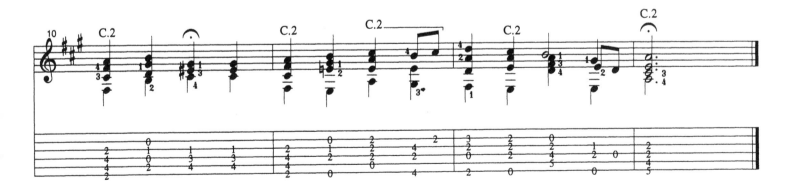

Prelude
for lute, BWV 999

Arranged for guitar by
Joseph Harris

J.S. Bach
(1685-1750)

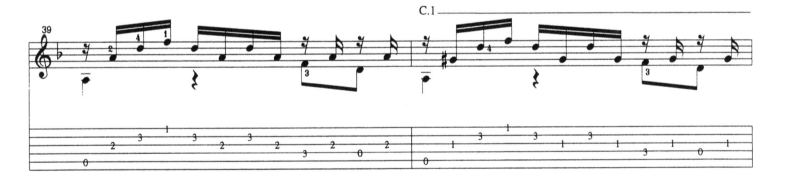

Bourrée
from Suite No. 1 for lute, BWV 996

Arranged for guitar by
Joseph Harris

J.S. Bach
(1685-1750)

Sarabande
from French Suite No. 1 for keyboard, BWV 812

Arranged for guitar by
Joseph Harris

J.S. Bach
(1685-1750)

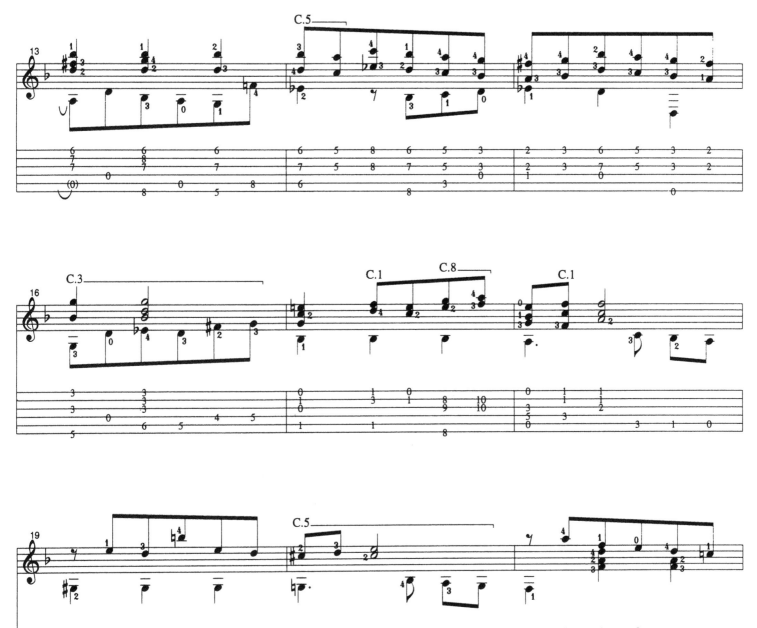

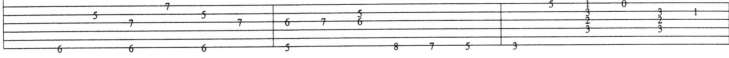

Sarabande
from Partita No. 1 for keyboard, BWV 825

Arranged for guitar by
Joseph Harris

J.S. Bach
(1685-1750)

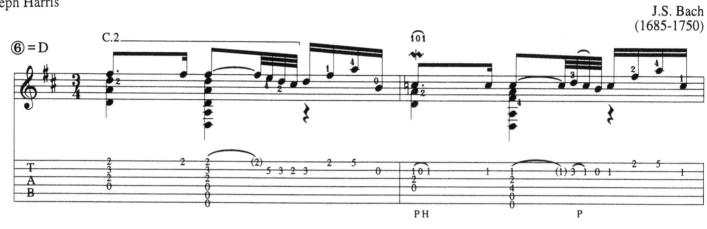

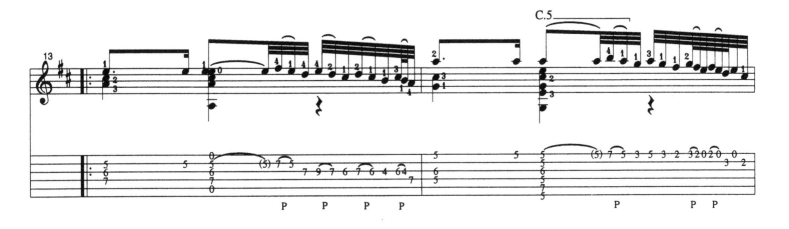

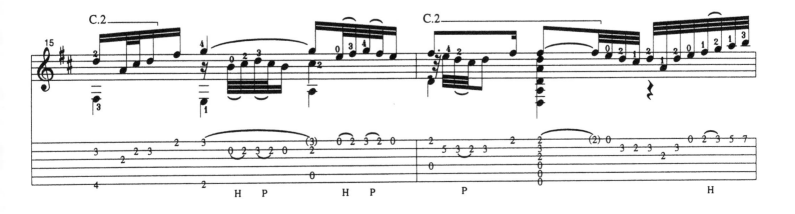

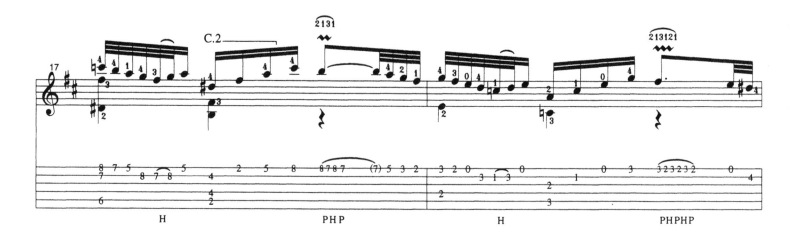

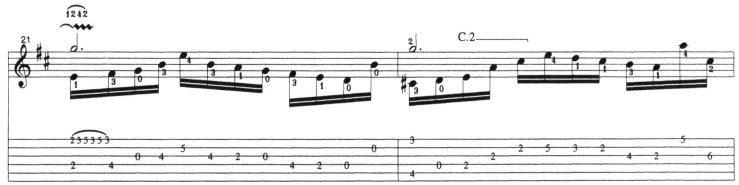

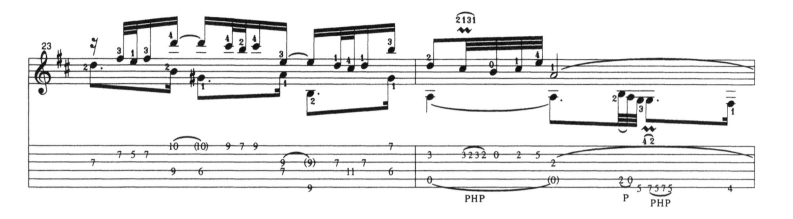

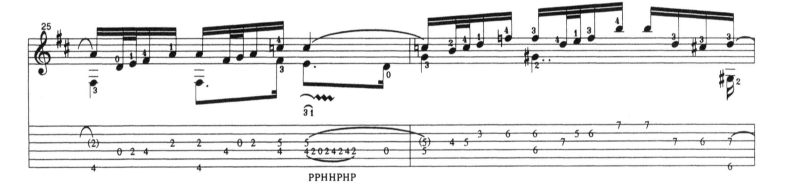

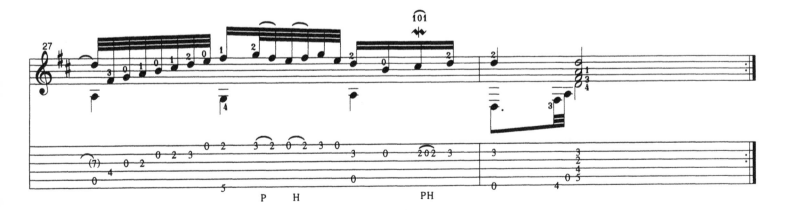

Musette in D Major
from the Notebook for Anna Magdalena Bach

Arranged for guitar by
Joseph Harris

J.S. Bach
(1685-1750)

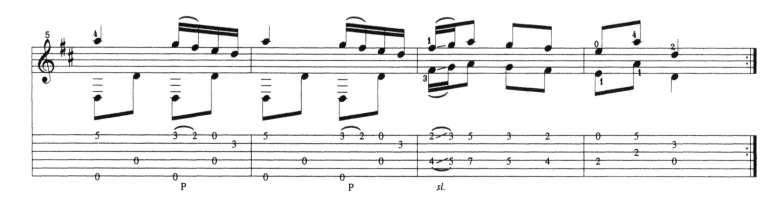

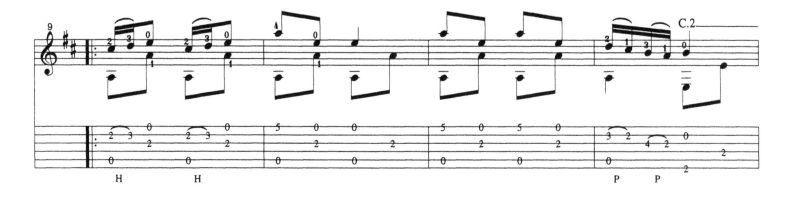

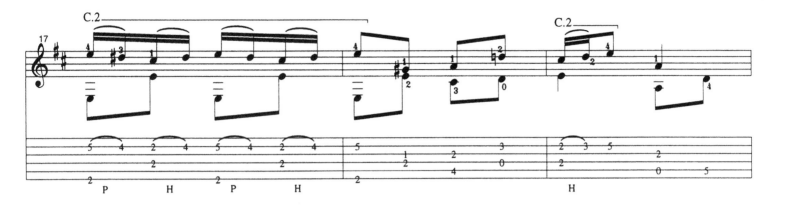

Sarabande
from Partita for Keyboard, HWV 454

Arranged for guitar
by Joseph Harris

George Frideric Handel
(1685-1759)

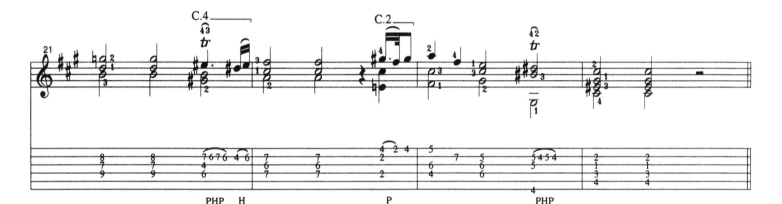

Andantino in C Major
from *Méthode complète pour la guitarre* (1840)

Edited and fingered by
Joseph Harris

Matteo Carcassi
(1792–1853)

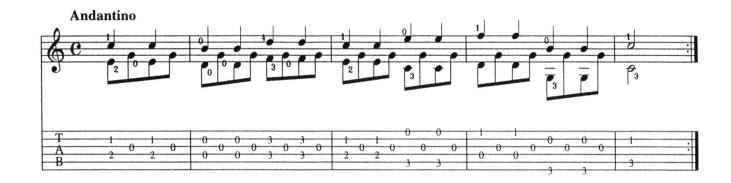

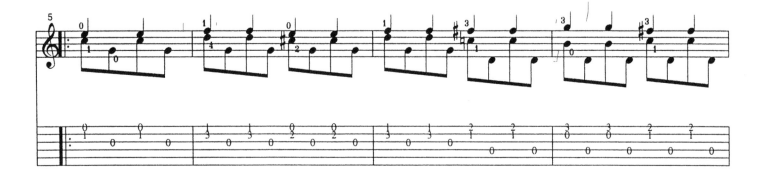

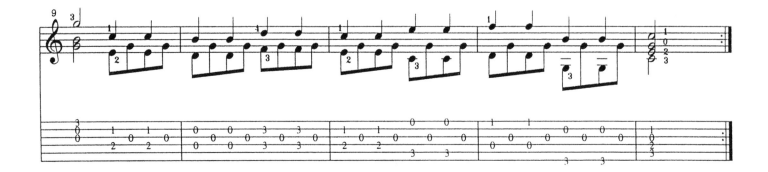

Study in A Minor
Op. 60, No. 7

Edited and fingered by
Joseph Harris

Matteo Carcassi
(1792–1853)

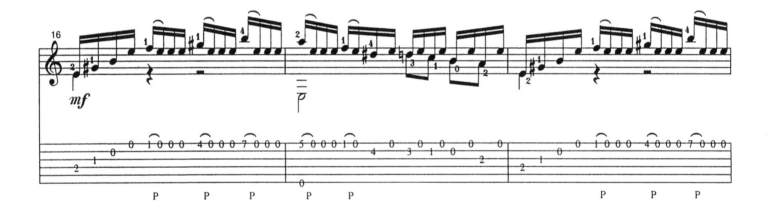

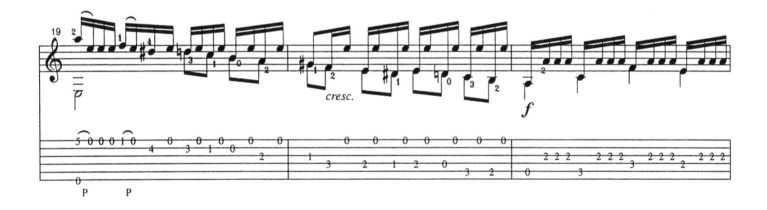

Prelude in C Major
from *Méthode complète pour la guitarre* (1840)

Edited and fingered by
Joseph Harris

Matteo Carcassi
(1792–1853)

Study in A Minor
from *Nuevo Método para Guitarra* (1843)

Edited and fingered by
Joseph Harris

Dionisio Aguado
(1784–1849)

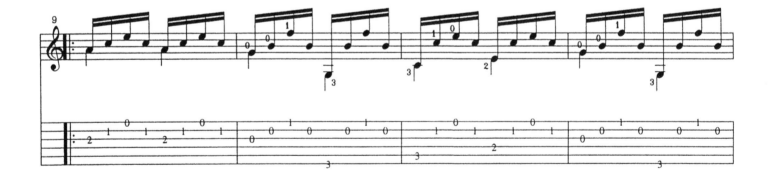

Minuet in G Major
Op. 2, No. 1

Edited and fingered by
Joseph Harris

Fernando Sor
(1788–1839)

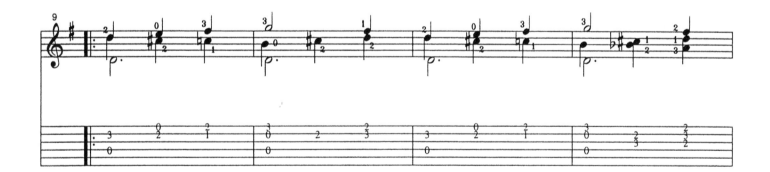

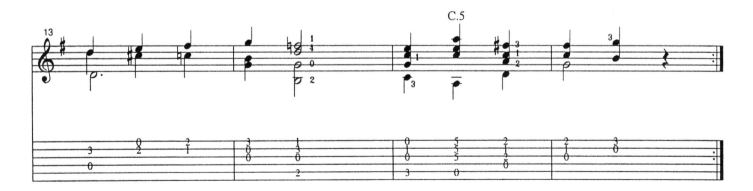

Leçon in D Major
Op. 31, No. 10

Edited and fingered by
Joseph Harris

Fernando Sor
(1778-1839)

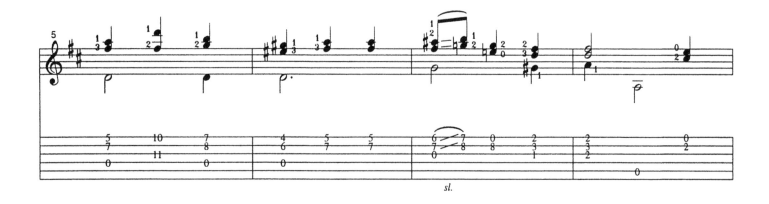

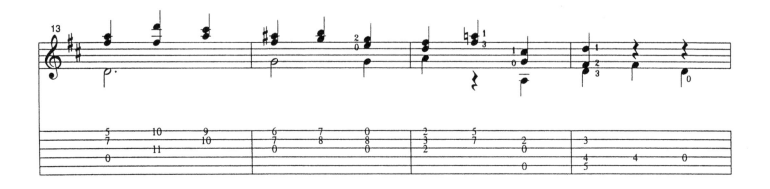

Leçon in E Major
Op. 31, No. 23

Edited and fingered by
Joseph Harris

Fernando Sor
(1778-1839)

Mouvement de prière religieuse

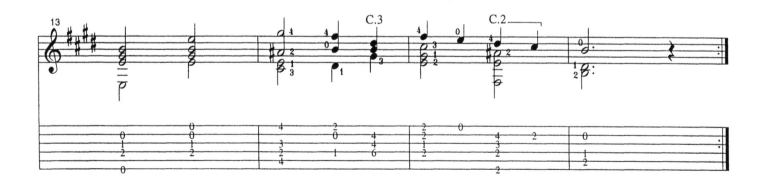

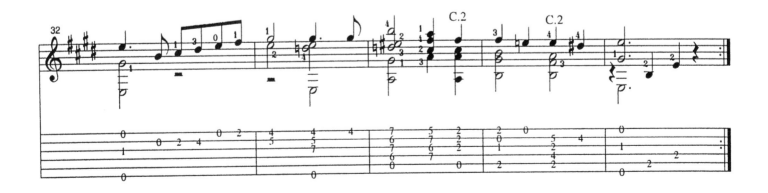

Petite Pièce in E Major
Op. 32, No. 1

Edited and fingered by
Joseph Harris

Fernando Sor
(1778-1839)

Andantino

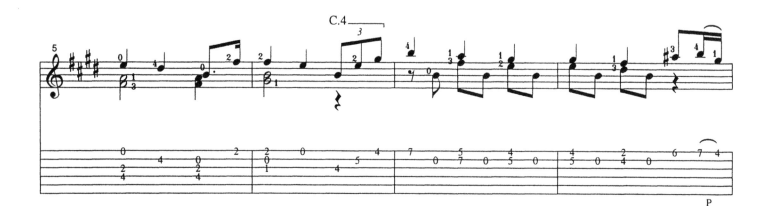

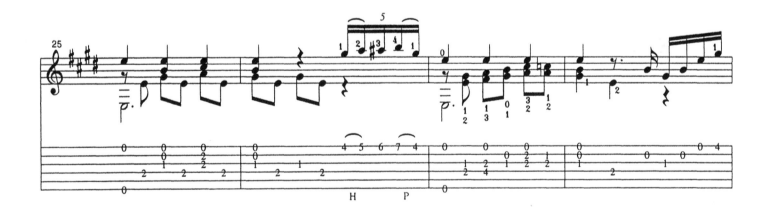

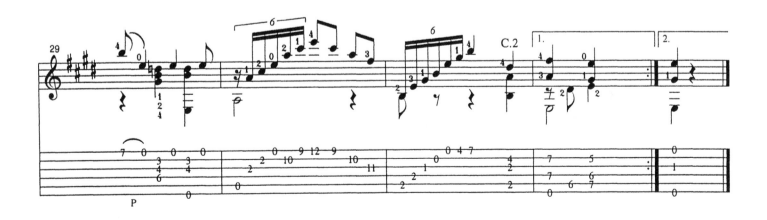

Petite Pièce in A Major
Op. 44, No. 21

Edited and fingered by
Joseph Harris

Fernando Sor
(1778-1839)

Study in B Minor
Op. 35, No. 22

Edited and fingered by
Joseph Harris

Fernando Sor
(1788–1839)

Study in C Major

Edited and fingered by
Joseph Harris

Francisco Tárrega
(1852–1909)

Lágrima
(Preludio)

Edited and fingered by
Joseph Harris

Francisco Tárrega
(1852–1909)

Adelita
(Mazurca)

Edited and fingered by
Joseph Harris

Francisco Tárrega
(1852–1909)

María
(Gavota)

Arranged for guitar by
Joseph Harris

Francisco Tárrega
(1852-1909)

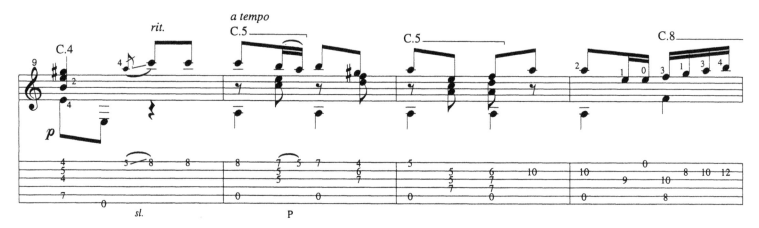

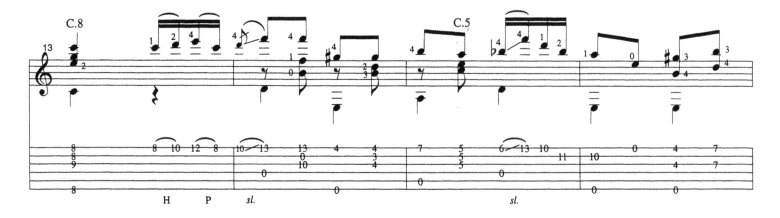

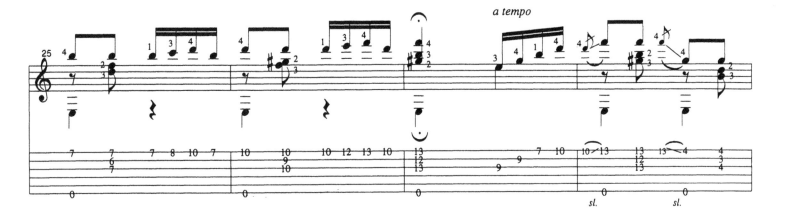

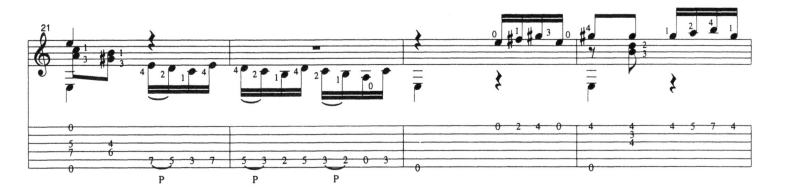

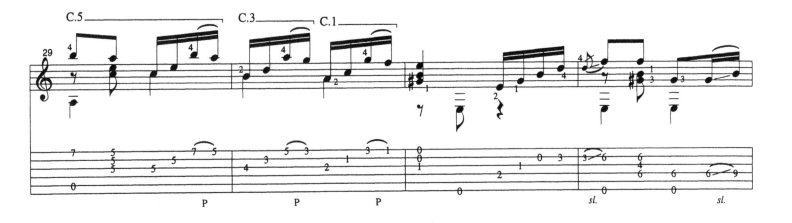

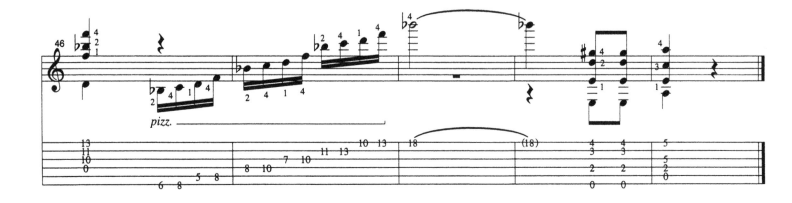

Canción Triste
from *Preludios Vascos*, Book I (1912)

Arranged for guitar by
Joseph Harris

P. José Antonio de Donostía
(1886-1957)

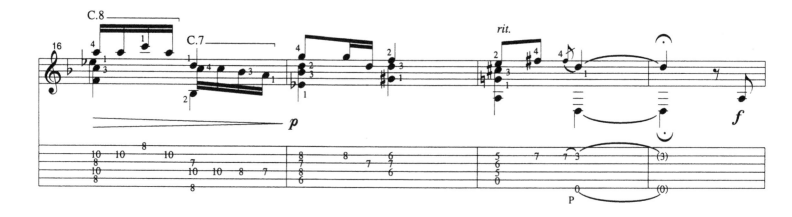

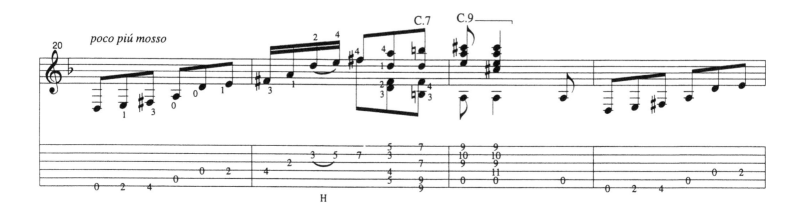

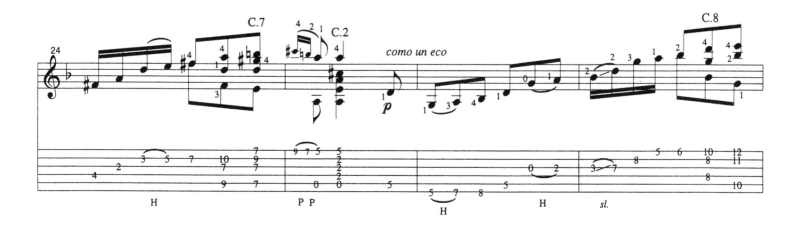

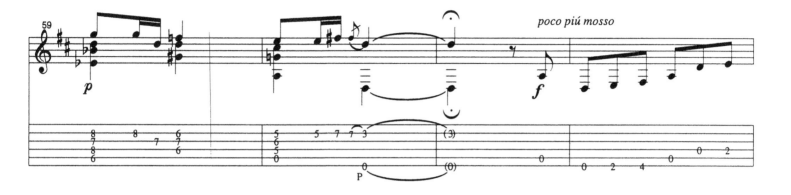

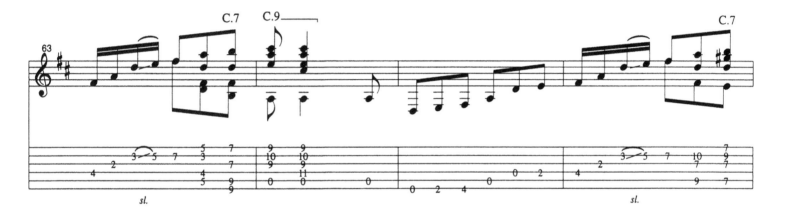

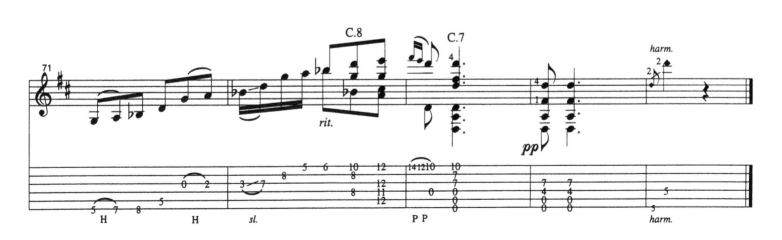

Romanza

Arranged for guitar by
Joseph Harris

traditional Spanish
folk melody

El Noi de la Mare

Arranged for guitar by
Joseph Harris

traditional Spanish
folk melody

El Mestre

Arranged for guitar by
Joseph Harris

traditional
arr. Joe Harris

Andante teneramente

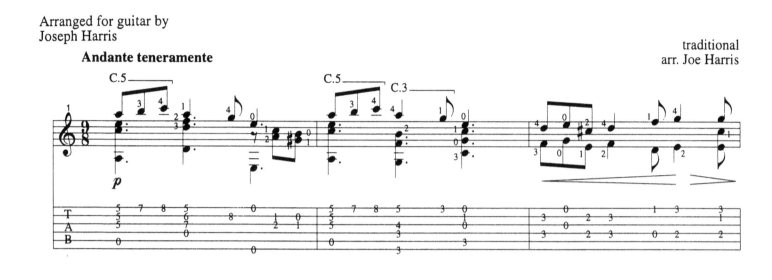

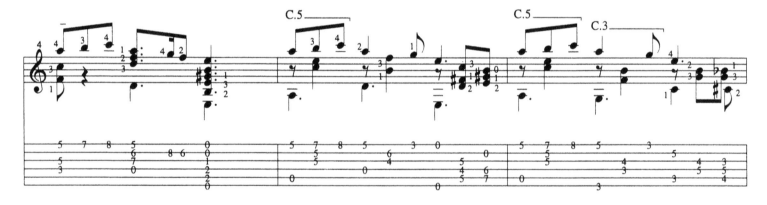

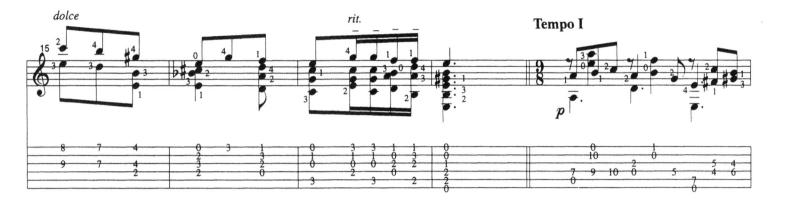

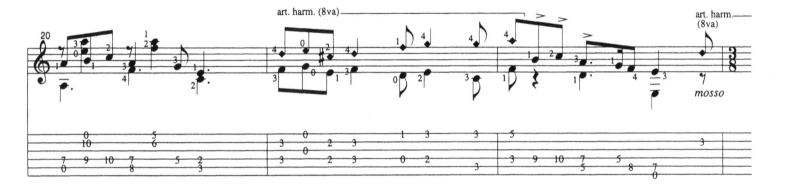

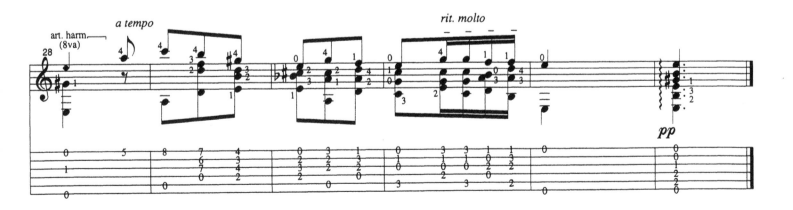

Danza Mora

Arranged for guitar by
Joseph Harris

Francisco Tárrega
(1852-1909)

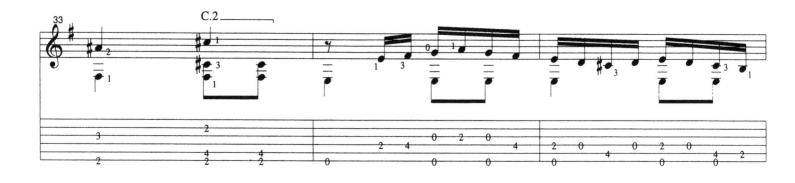

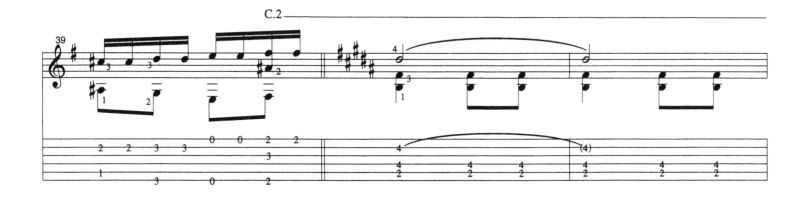

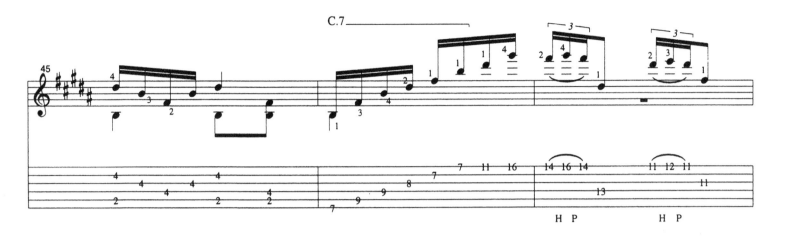

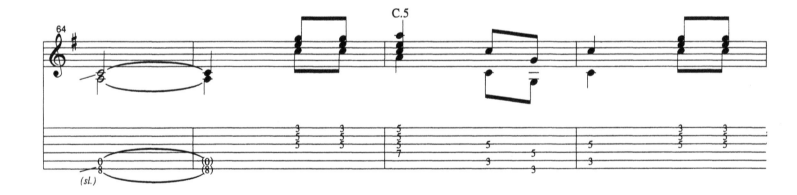

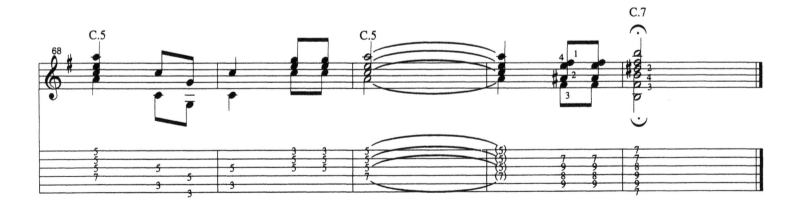